Help Your Child with Numeracy

Also available from Continuum

Developmental Approach to Early Numeracy, Carol Aubrey

Numeracy Activities KS2, Afzal Ahmed and Honor Williams

Numeracy Activities KS3, Afzal Ahmed, Honor Williams and George Wickham

Mathematics at Home, John Davies

Parent's Guide to Primary School, Katy Byrne and Harvey McGavin

Help Your Child to Succeed, Bill Lucas and Alistair Smith

Help Your Child to Succeed Toolkit, Bill Lucas and Alistair Smith

Help Your Young Child to Succeed, Ros Bayley, Lynn Broadbent and Debbie Pullinger

Getting Your Little Darlings to Behave, Sue Cowley

Help Your Talented Child, Barry Teare

Help Your Child with Numeracy

Rosemary Russell

continuum

Continuum International Publishing Group
The Tower Building, 11 York Road, London SE1 7NX
80 Maiden Lane, Suite 704, New York, NY 10038

www.continuumbooks.com

British Library Cataloguing-in-Publication Data
A catalogue record for this book is available from the British Library.

ISBN: 0-8264-9573-7 (paperback)

Library of Congress Cataloging-in-Publication Data
A catalog record for this book is available from the Library of Congress

Designed and typeset by Kenneth Burnley, Wirral, Cheshire
Printed and bound in Great Britain by Ashford Colour Press,
Gosport, Hampshire

Contents

Introduction

Maths is good for you!

Research has shown that:

■ Numeracy exercises are very good for the brain

■ In the long term, this helps employment prospects
■ Maths qualifications can lead to more earning power

How this book will help

It will:

■ Secure your knowledge
■ Give you ideas of how to help
■ Provide exercises (Workouts!) to do with your child

- Show you what schools are trying to do
- Tell you what children are expected to learn at a given age
- Lead you to more resources

The most important help – providing the right environment

As a parent, your love, care and support has possibly the biggest positive influence on your child's achievement. Make sure they have a good diet, which includes fruit and vegetables, and are getting enough sleep. Let them enjoy a mixture of social activities. Have a laugh with them. Organize trips out like going swimming, visiting places of interest or going to the theatre. Having this balance is important, especially during exam times when they are older.

Everyday maths

Making maths part of everyday life is one of the best ways for children to feel confident in using and working with numbers.

For example, with younger children, counting is very important: How many teddies on the shelf? How many apples in the bag? Then working out one more, two more and three more than the number helps mathematical thinking.

Practise matching objects and getting over the concept 'same as': Please fetch me a spoon the same as this. Use words which communicate comparisons: Which is the tallest/shortest tree?

...3...4...5...
6...7...8...9...

For older children, shopping gives many opportunities for practising numeracy skills. Look out for offers: Buy two get the third free. Work out with them how much each item costs, and how much has been saved.

Start from where they are

Be sensitive when a child gets something wrong. Don't just say, 'You've got that wrong, this is how you do it.' Instead, start from where they're at and ask them, 'Tell me, how did you get that answer?' As they discuss things with you, areas of misunderstanding and so on will become clear. Then show them where they went wrong, and help them to correct the mistake.

Often, they have misunderstood or half-learnt a procedure, or they do not understand certain mathematical words or symbols (see the Glossary at back of book). It could be that they have just misread the question!

Lots of ways to learn

There is no single, exclusively correct learning style in maths. We learn things in a variety of ways, so help children to learn by using two or more of their senses, e.g. hearing as well as seeing. Older children can make use of a multisensory approach to learning multiplication facts (tables):

- Write out tables
- Draw arrays or groups of objects
- Learn tables to a rhythm or rap
- Cover the tables over
- Write down the multiplication facts
- Check what you have written

Some of the methods used to teach the basics such as addition and subtraction may come as a surprise. Hopefully this book will help you to recognize what is going on, and the thinking behind it, so you can work alongside school, and not confuse your child. If you are unsure, do ask the teacher.

Keep in touch with the teacher, and don't be afraid to discuss any concerns you may have. Remember to pass on any good news too!

Praise and encouragement – building self-esteem

It is tremendously important to praise what is right, and not focus only on mistakes. If there has been a lot of failure at maths, a child's self-esteem can be brought down and this does not help them to learn. So, encourage them to ask questions if they don't understand, and reassure them that no question is too simple to ask. They may need another type of explanation, so be ready to give that. Remind them that other people probably have the same problem, but don't have the courage to ask. If they get stuck, backtrack to the point where they did understand, and start from there. Build self-esteem by encouraging them that these are quite common experiences. The key is to celebrate what is right!

Great expectations – but not too great!

Good maths is built on solid foundations, and these take time to settle. It is very important to develop mental arithmetic skills, even though calculators do exist. Be patient. Be aware that there is a huge gap between the very important early stages of informal, mental arithmetic and the formal, written methods that adults expect to see. Don't try to jump too quickly!

Note that many of the Workouts in this book indicate the school year in which children will meet that work.

Using practice books can be helpful, as long as sessions are not too long and the tasks are appropriate for the child's age. Some are recommended in Appendix 2.

Remember that children learn at different rates.

Schools

National Curriculum

The National Curriculum describes what children are to be taught. It applies to all students of compulsory school age in maintained schools in England.

Key Stages

The National Curriculum is organized broadly into what are known as Key Stages. The pupils' age dictates which Key Stage they belong to. A rough guide to the ages is as follows:

Key Stage 1	5–7 years old	Year groups 1–2
Key Stage 2	7–11 years old	Year groups 3–6
Key Stage 3	11–14 years old	Year groups 7–9
Key Stage 4	14–16 years old	Year groups 10–11

Numeracy Strategy

In September 1999, the government introduced in primary schools the National Numeracy Strategy to help raise standards in mathematics for all primary-aged pupils, and this has since been renewed. The National Curriculum says *what* is to be taught, whereas the 'Strategy' (or the 'Framework') gives guidance on *how* mathematics is to be taught.

Primary schoolchildren often spend about an hour each day (between 45 and 60 minutes, depending on their age) learning mathematics, and so their lessons are often known as the Numeracy Hour.

There is a lot of emphasis on mental calculations at first. Once these are secure, children are introduced to standard written methods. Using the correct mathematical vocabulary is important too.

Typical lessons

Their lessons are usually split into three parts:

The oral/mental starter: this lasts approximately 10 minutes, and the children are taught together. It is time to practise skills.

The main teaching activity: this lasts about 30 to 40 minutes. Children may work in groups for this part.

The plenary: the last 10 minutes or so are spent with the whole class together, discussing and finding out what the children have learnt. The teacher might also use this time to remind students of the important points of the lesson.

SATs and assessment

Throughout the year teachers are continually assessing students to monitor their progress and use the information to help plan suitable work. At the end of each Key Stage, when children are about 7, 11 and 14 years old, those who attend maintained schools in England are required to take tests, commonly known as SATs.

At Key Stages 2 and 3 (for children aged approximately 11 and 14), these tests are taken in May and are sent off to be externally marked. At Key Stage 1 (for children aged approximately 7), the teacher uses suitable tests, and marks them and has the flexibility to choose when to set them.

The children's results are given in the form of a level (see below). You will be sent a report informing you what level your child is working at.

Levels

Each 'level' roughly describes what sort of things a child is capable of doing in a particular subject. They start at Level 1 and work upwards. So to be at Level 3, a child would have to progress through Level 1 and Level 2, which is further split into sections which start at 2c, then 2b and 2a. Most children by the age of 7 are working at Level 2.

Appendix 2 gives a gist of the sort of thing your child should be able to do by the end of school years Reception, Year 1 and Year 2.

Remember, do not worry if they seem ahead in some areas and not so strong in others. Children learn at different rates.

Basic numeracy

Units, tens, hundreds and thousands

Our number system is a very simple, clever and elegant structure that allows us to write down very complicated arithmetic with very few symbols. Understanding how it works is the key to everything.

We arrange our numbers in tens. We begin counting things with the digits 1, 2, 3, 4, 5, 6, 7, 8 and 9, and these are called Units. After nine, we say 'ten' and write it as 10; the 1 on the left means one group of Ten and the 0 ('nought' or 'zero') on the right shows that there are no Units.

The next number is eleven: 1 Ten and 1 Unit, 11. We then go up through the Units again: 12, 13, 14 . . . up to 19. After 19 we have twenty: 2 Tens and 0 Units, 20. So we go on until we get to 99; after this, we have 10 Tens (which we call a Hundred), no other Tens and no Units, 100.

The beauty of it is that we can keep on doing this indefinitely: every time we reach ten, we can start a new column to the left. So with only ten digits (0–9) we can write down any number, no matter how big. The position of each digit tells us how much it is worth: this is its Place Value.

Extract from our number system

Thousands (1000)	Hundreds (100)	Tens (10)	Units (1)
	8	0	5
2	0	3	0

The number eight hundred and five would be written as 8 in the hundreds column, there are no tens (i.e. no twenty, thirty, etc.) so zero is placed in the tens column, and there are five units so 5 is placed in the units column.

$$8 \times 100 \quad = \quad 800$$

$$0 \times 10 \quad = \quad 0$$

$$5 \times 1 \quad = \quad 5$$

Adding together gives:

$$
\begin{array}{r}
800 \\
0 \\
+\ 5 \\
\hline
805
\end{array}
$$

In the number two thousand and thirty, there are two thousands, so 2 is placed in the thousands column, no hundreds, so zero is placed in the hundreds column, thirty (which is three tens) is represented by 3 in the tens column, and no units, so zero is placed in the units column. (See table above.)

In any whole number, the value of the units column must be shown (even if it is zero). By its position we can work out the value of the other digits.

Starting off

It is important that children know the number names, and be able to recite them in order, from and back to zero. Certain nursery rhymes are useful for this. For example, in Reception they may join in and sing, 'Ten green bottles . . .' and 'One man went to mow . . .' It is also very helpful practising saying, forwards and backwards, sequences such as the multiples of 10 up to 100:

Zero, ten, twenty, thirty . . . , one hundred

They need to be able to count reliably a set of objects.

Workout 1

1. What number comes (i) after 7? (ii) after 15? (iii) before 8? (Year 1)

2. Which tens number comes (i) after 60? (ii) before 40? (Year 2)

3. Ask them to fetch four spoons, four plates. (Year 1)

Children learn to read and write numbers up to at least 20 in Year 1, up to at least 100 in Year 2, and up to at least 1000 in Year 3.

Workout 2

Try writing out these numbers in figures:

1. Seventy-two

2. One hundred and fifty-six

3. Three hundred and six

4. Nine hundred and fourteen

In classes, because it is very important to realize how numbers are formed, children use place value cards to help see how a number is made up. They 'partition' (split up) a number into 100s, 10s and units. For example, twelve is a ten and a two.

Workout 3

1. Have some 10p coins and 1p coins to hand. Ask them to give you eighteen pence in 10p and 1p coins. (Year 1)

2. Explain what number needs to go in each box

   (i)   83 = [   ] + 3

   (ii) 54 = 50 + [   ] (Year 2)

3. Explain what number needs to go into each box

   (i)   547 = [   ] + 40 + 7

   (ii) 639 = 600 + [   ] + 9 (Year 3)

4. Make the biggest and smallest numbers you can with these digits:

   8, 2, 3 (Year 3)

5. Write the number that is the same as eight thousands, seven hundreds, five tens and six ones. (Year 4)

6. What does the digit 5 in 56 represent? And the 6? (Year 2)

Rewriting a number in smaller units

An important numeracy skill is to be able to rewrite a number in smaller units. Here are some examples. ONE hundred is the same as TEN tens, or ONE HUNDRED units. So 500 is the same as FIFTY tens (ten tens equals one hundred, so twenty tens equals two hundred . . . so fifty tens equals five hundred). ONE thousand is TEN hundreds.

1. How many tens in 230?
2. How many hundreds in 4800?
3. Which is more, 81 tens or 8 hundreds? (Year 4)

Number lines

It is very important to be able to order numbers. Seeing a number line, showing the numbers in their correct order, helps to do this. Rulers are a good visual example of a number line. They are sometimes used in this way as a number line, for things like checking addition.

Blank (or empty) number lines are also used as an aid in addition and subtraction. These are just straight lines, with no markings on them. It is up to the person doing the addition or subtraction to decide on the position of the important, landmark numbers to help with the calculation. They are not drawn to scale.

For example:

24 + 48

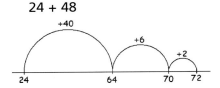

Mentally, the 48 is split up (partitioned) into suitable parts, and there are various ways this can be done.

48 = 40 + 6 + 2   or

48 = 10 + 10 + 10 + 10 + 6 + 2   etc.

The addition is then done by jottings using an empty number line, with arches above, and labels.

Since it does not matter the order in which you do an addition, you could start with the 48 and add on 24. (Year 3)

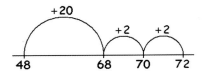

It is very helpful to use ordinary, everyday situations to practise mental additions by partitioning numbers.

Workout 5

1. Shuffle some playing cards (use numbers 2 to 9), and ask your child to put them in order. (Year 1)

2. Two numbers are out of order. Put them right:

   11, 12, 15, 14, 13, 16   (Year 1)

3. Put these lengths in order, largest first:

   12mm, 8mm, 22mm, 4mm, 15mm   (Year 1)

4. Put these in order, smallest amount first:

   £2.20, £8.80, £3.30, £5.80, £2.50   (Year 3)

5. Use an empty number line to add 33 + 59. (Year 3)

Addition

Knowing number facts and doubling and halving

It is very useful to know by heart all the addition and subtraction facts for all numbers up to and including 5 by the end of Year 1; up to 10 by the end of Year 2; and up to 20 by the end of Year 3.

For example, know the pairs for 11:

$1 + 10 = 11$ $10 + 1 = 11$ $2 + 9 = 11$ $9 + 2 = 11$, etc.

$11 - 1 = 10$ $11 - 10 = 1$ $11 - 2 = 9$ $11 - 9 = 2$, etc.

Using known facts to work out the addition doubles of numbers up to twenty, e.g. $17 + 17 = 34$, makes a good basis for helping with addition.

Let your child have plenty of practice with addition facts, using number lines, and 10p and 1p coins.

Workout 6

1. Show 3 apples. How many more apples are needed to make 10?   (Year 1)

2. With a pair of dice, I roll double 6. What is my score?   (Year 2)

3. Put numbers in the boxes to total 20:

    (i)   [   ] + 3 = 20

    (ii) [   ] + [   ] = 20   (Year 2)

4. 95 + 95 = [   ]   (Year 3)

5. What is a half of 34?   (Year 3)

Respect different strategies used

Remember, there are various ways that an addition calculation can be worked out.

For example, 4 + 5:

- You could count on 5 starting from 4 . . . 5, 6, 7, 8, 9
- You could count on 4 starting from 5 . . . 6, 7, 8, 9
- You could remember your doubles: 5 is 4 + 1; 4 + 4 = 8, + 1 more to make 9
- Remember your number facts: 4 + 5 = 9

Don't force a particular way for your child to do a calculation. Ask them to explain how they calculate a sum. It is good for them to learn how to do this.

Vocabulary

There are many expressions used that mean work out an addition. Here are some:

- What is the total of 7 and 11?
- Add 7 and 11.
- What is the sum of 7 and 11?
- 7 plus 11 makes . . . ?

Stages in teaching addition – paper and pencil procedures

There is a lot of mental arithmetic in class, but eventually (maybe not until Year 3) all children need to learn how to write down their calculations.

At first, additions sums are simple and written out in a line. The next stage is to learn how to write them in a vertical layout, and do the calculation. Children are asked first how they mentally work out the calculation, and try to write that down. For example:

$$74 + 58 = (70 + 50) + (4 + 8) = 120 + 12 = 132 \quad \text{or}$$

$$74 + 58 = (4 + 8) + (70 + 50) = 12 + 120 = 132$$

Children move towards a vertical layout showing the same way they mentally carried out the calculations, making sure numbers are lined up in their correct place value.

They would be told that the vertical layout is a more organized way of writing their mental calculations.

Adding the tens first, or   Adding units first,
then the units   then the tens

```
      74                        74
    + 58                      + 58
    ────                      ────
     120                        12
      12                       120
    ────                      ────
     132                       132
```

At this stage, they are then told that when writing down calculations, it is important to start with adding the units first.

By the end of Year 3, children will have moved towards 'carrying' below the line, at first using numbers they are confident with. Both layouts would be shown side by side. For example:

```
      57                        57
    + 26                      + 26
    ────                      ────
      13                        83
      70                        1
    ────
      83
```

There is a gradual progression. At first, no tens or hundreds need to be carried, and then calculations get more difficult. For example, 346 + 87:

$$
\begin{array}{r}
346 \\
+\ 87 \\
\hline
13 \\
120 \\
300 \\
\hline
433
\end{array}
\qquad
\begin{array}{r}
346 \\
+\ 87 \\
\hline
433 \\
\text{\small 1 1}
\end{array}
$$

Before working out the sum, children are encouraged to estimate the size of their answer, and then check to see if their answer is reasonable.

Workout 7   Add these numbers using the expanded layout and the compressed layout:

(i) 58 + 35   (ii) 765 + 73

Subtraction

Many methods

As we have seen, the work on subtraction is very much linked with the work on addition. There are many ways to calculate a subtraction. Here are some.

Links with number facts

Children learn number facts up to 20 by Year 3, so they are learning the pairs of numbers that make up to 20. You can help them with subtraction by encouraging the links with addition. For example, 11 take away 8 equals something, is the same as, 8 plus something makes 11.

Counting on or complementary addition – 'the shopkeepers' method'

When we calculate a subtraction, we are working out the gap between two numbers. You can find this gap by counting on. The answer to 11 take away 8, is the same as the answer to counting on from 8 to make 11. An empty number line is useful to calculate this. This method is often used when giving change, and is also known as 'the shopkeepers' method'.

For example:

11 – 8

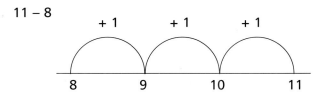

The gap is three. Therefore, 11 – 8 = 3.

Another example:

45 − 23

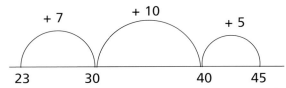

So add the steps 7 + 10 + 5 to get the answer of 22.

Counting back down – it's different

Counting on involves starting with the smaller number. We could also count 23 back down from 45 to find the answer, 22. In this way, we start with the larger number, placed on the right of the number line, and look for the landmark numbers in the same way, this time labelling the arches with negative numbers instead, working from right to left. We arrive at the answer 22 on the number line.

Workout 8

Work out 76 − 29 using the shopkeepers' method on a number line. Try also counting back down using a number line.

Rounding and compensating

If we think of 9p as 1p less than 10p, and 99p as 1p less than £1, etc., it helps us to calculate bills quickly. We would round to the nearest pound, then compensate by taking off the extra pennies we added on at the end of the calculation.

For example:

£3.99 + £2.99 = £4 − 1p + £3 − 1p = £7 − 2p = £6.98

Vocabulary

There are many words and expressions used to mean work out a subtraction. Ask questions that use a variety of these:

Subtract, take (away), minus, find the difference between . . . and . . . How many are left/left over? How many fewer is . . . than . . . ? How many more is . . . than . . . ?

■ I had 34 apples, and gave 17 away. How many are left?

■ What is the difference between 17 and 34?

■ What is 34 minus 17?

Stages in teaching subtraction

There is plenty of practice of subtraction using mental methods, number lines and jottings and rounding and compensating. However, to cope with harder subtractions, children need to learn how to write down calculations.

Easier subtractions

At first, as with addition, subtractions are written out in lines. Children would then move to a vertical format. Beginning with numbers they can cope with mentally, they write them out in an expanded form, making sure that numbers are lined up in their correct place value. Children need to be guided to get into the habit of starting the subtraction with the units.

For example, 86 – 53:

$$
\begin{array}{r}
(80 + 6) \\
- (50 + 3) \\
\hline
(30 + 3) = 33
\end{array}
\qquad
\begin{array}{r}
\text{leads to} \quad 86 \\
- 53 \\
\hline
33
\end{array}
$$

or 672 – 251:

$$
\begin{array}{r}
(600 + 70 + 2) \\
- (200 + 50 + 1) \\
\hline
(400 + 20 + 1) = 421
\end{array}
\qquad
\begin{array}{r}
\text{leads to} \quad 672 \\
- 251 \\
\hline
421
\end{array}
$$

Harder subtractions

For example, 47 – 29:

$$
\begin{array}{r}
(40 + 7) \\
- (20 + 9)
\end{array}
$$

As you can see, in the units column we cannot immediately perform the subtraction because we cannot take 9 away from 7.

Now, not many people know that there is more than one written method of subtracting. This can cause a lot of confusion and argument. Here are the two main methods. They are both correct, but you must not mix them up!

$$
\begin{array}{r}
\overset{3}{\cancel{4}}{}^{1}7 \\
- 29 \\
\hline
18
\end{array}
$$

Subtraction by Decomposition

Subtraction by Equal Addition

$$
\begin{array}{r}
4\,{}^{1}7 \\
- 2\,\underset{1}{9} \\
\hline
18
\end{array}
$$

Subtraction by decomposition:

The first method of subtraction is called subtraction by decomposition. This is the more commonly taught method in schools today.

We can use coins to show how to work it out.

If I have 4 × 10p and 7 × 1p coins, I have 47p; but if I have 3 × 10p and 17 × 1p coins, I also have 47p. So to solve my subtraction I can change one of my 10p coins into 10 × 1p.

$$\begin{array}{r} {}^{-1\ +10} \\ 47 \\ -\ 29 \\ \hline \end{array}$$

Seven take away nine is not possible, so . . .

(i)   I change one of the tens in the tens column of the top number into ten units: I 'decompose' it, just like changing a ten pence piece into ten pennies.

$$\begin{array}{r} {}^{3}\!\!\diagdown \\ 4\,{}^{1}7 \\ -\ 29 \\ \hline 18 \end{array}$$

(ii) This leaves three tens in the tens column, and we add the ten units to the units column.

(iii) Ten units plus seven makes seventeen in the units column, and nine from seventeen is eight.

(iv) In the tens column, three tens take away two tens leaves one ten.

Subtraction by equal addition:

This method uses the fact that the difference between two numbers does not change if you add the same number to both. We can add 10 to each number, and the difference between 39 and 57 is just the same as the difference between 29 and 47. We can see this on the 'number line':

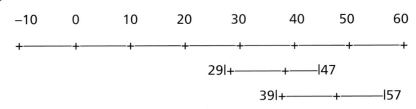

Remember that we write our numbers in columns, and each column has a value.

By adding 10 to the 29 as normal (making 39) and adding 10 to the 47 in the units column (making 57 but thinking of as it 'forty-seventeen'), we can now do the subtraction easily.

$$\begin{array}{r} 4\,^{1}7 \\ -\ 29 \\ _{1} \\ \hline 18 \end{array}$$

The example on the right shows you how. 9 from 17 is 8, and 3 tens from 4 tens is 1 ten.

NB: You might know this as the 'borrow and pay back' method, but that is a really confusing description. Think of it as giving the same to both numbers!

Please remember that although both methods are valid, they are quite different, so do not mix them up!

Please check which method your child is being taught at school and stick to that.

Fractions and decimals

In mathematics, fractions and decimals are parts of a whole. In schools the approach to the teaching about fractions and decimals in the early years is through lots of practical and visual work.

There is a lot more to fractions than at first meets the eye. To start with, we use special symbols for fractions. Children do not start adding, subtracting, multiplying and dividing fractions until much later on. In the early years, it is vitally important that they grasp the idea of what a fraction is. As a parent you can contribute enormously by helping your child, as they go about their daily activities, to recognize fractions.

Background on fractions

In everyday life, we use the word fraction to mean something smaller. For example, 'I bought this belt at a fraction of the price' – means that you have got a bargain, and paid a smaller price than usual. Fractions have a similar meaning in mathematics except when you split something into fractions, either an item such as a cake, or an amount such as 30p, you split whatever you start with into smaller equal parts. Halving is splitting the something into two equal parts; splitting into thirds means splitting the something into three equal parts.

The important thing is for children to recognize what is meant by a fraction. They start with the simple ones, such as halves and quarters. Activities such as cooking are an excellent way of seeing hands-on what half of a quantity looks like. When baking a Victoria sponge, about half the mixture goes in one tin, the other half in another.

It is important too for children to recognize what is not a half, and this can be seen when dividing, say, a whole pizza into two unequal parts.

Writing fractions

We use special symbols to show a fraction.

A half is written $^1/_2$. The bottom number (the denominator) tells you the number of equal parts, the top number (the numerator) tells you how many of these equal parts you want. So using our example, halving a cake means splitting the cake into two, each piece is $^1/_2$ a cake. Halving 30p would mean we have 2 lots of 15p.

Here is another example: find $^2/_3$ of 30p. We know from the denominator we need to split the amount into 3 equal parts, so $^1/_3$ of 30p is 10p. We want $^2/_3$ so two of these equal parts gives a total of 20p.

How fractions are taught in schools

In schools children gradually progress to identifying $^1/_2$ and $^1/_4$, and dividing quantities into 2 then 4 equal parts, then to being able to begin to estimate the sizes of fractions used in Year 3.

Activities that help them do this are: by practically making full turns and then, say, half a turn to the right in PE lessons, or moving the minute hand of a clock through one turn and talk about times like 'half past 4'.

Workout 10

1. What fraction is shaded? (Year 2)

2. Ring a quarter of the nuts. (Year 2)

   θ   θ
   θ   θ   θ   θ
   θ   θ

3. This bar is divided into two pieces, but they are not halves. Why not? (Year 2)

4. (i) Shade in $\frac{1}{10}$. (ii) What fraction is left not shaded? (Year 3)

Decimals

Children are introduced to decimals when they are older, in about Year 4.

Decimal fractions, to give them their full name, are fractions with denominators 10, 100, 1000, etc. We use a special notation to write these fractions, called decimal notation, and write $^1/_{10}$ as 0.1, $^1/_{100}$ as 0.01, etc.

As a parent you can contribute enormously in Key Stage 1 by helping your child to recognize decimals.

One way to do this is to take them shopping. Discuss with them the price of things. If the item costs £6.45, point out that it means 6 whole pounds plus some more. The cost is between £6 and £7.

Measuring using metric units such as metres is another way you can help to introduce decimals. (See Chapters on measuring and money.)

Multiplication and division

Leading on from addition and subtraction, multiplication and division are two important processes that children need to master.

What is multiplication?

One of the simplest ways to understand multiplication is as repeated addition. For example:

$4 + 4 + 4 = 12$,

or 4 multiplied by 3 is 12.

We use the symbol × to mean 'multiplied by', written $4 \times 3 = 12$, or we can say 3 lots of 4 equals 12, 4 times 3 is 12.

Another way is describing multiplication as an array. For example:

◆   ◆   ◆   ◆

◆   ◆   ◆   ◆ 4×3

◆   ◆   ◆   ◆

3×4

Here we can see that a multiplication can be calculated in any order as:

$3 \times 4 = 4 \times 3 = 12$.

This is very important.

Yet another way is seeing multiplication as a scaling factor, e.g., build a row using 3 bricks, now make another row 5 times as long. You would have to use 15 bricks as $3 \times 5 = 15$.

Children are taught these three different ways of seeing multiplication.

Vocabulary

There are many expressions used to mean work out a multiplication. Here are some:

- 3 lots of 4 (4×3)
- 4 times 3 (3×4)
- Multiply 3 by 4 (3×4)
- 3 groups of 4 (4×3)
- 3 times as big $(. . . \times 3)$

Please note: '4 times 3' could mean 'four, taken three times' or 'three, taken four times', fortunately the answer, 12, as we have seen, is the same for both. A multiplication can be calculated in any order!

You can help enormously by practising:

- Counting in 2s up to 20
- Counting in 10s up to 50
- Counting in 5s up to 20 (Year 1)

Help your child know by heart:

- The 2 times table up to 2×10
- The 10 times table up to 10×10 (Year 2)
- By asking them rapid questions, such as, 6 times 2? (12)

 Workout 11

1. How many wheels are there on 3 cars? (Year 2)
2. Double 8. (Year 2)
3. Twice 40? (Year 2)
4. Sara's pencil is 4cm long. Sally's pencil is twice as long. How long is Sally's pencil? (Year 2)

What is division?

Division and multiplication are what are known as inverse operations. Put simply, they 'undo' each other. Addition and subtraction are also inverse operations. First let's see how they 'undo' each other, so that we can understand an inverse operation. Children learn and use the words 'inverse operations' in about Year 4.

For example, starting with 4, then add 3, we get 7. But, 7 minus 3 gets us back to 4, the number we started with. The subtraction undoes the addition.

Written out, it looks like this: 4 + 3 = 7, and 7 − 3 = 4.

Now let's look at division and multiplication. If we start with 3 multiplied by 4 we get 12. If we divide 12 by 4 we get 3, the number we started with.

Written out, it looks like this: 3 × 4 = 12, and 12 ÷ 4 = 3.

Appendix 1 gives a multiplication square showing all the times tables up to 10 × 10. Using the example given, you can see how it can be used for a division as well as for a multiplication. Children would use the multiplication square and do this sort of work much later on in Key Stage 2, in about Year 5.

The target in Key Stage 1 is for children to begin to use the division symbol, ÷, sometime in Year 2, and learn that we can see division in two ways:

1. Sharing equally

Here is an example of seeing division as sharing equally between groups:

8 conkers are shared equally between 2 people, how many does each get?

To work this out, we calculate the division: 8 ÷ 2 = 4. Each gets 4.

2. Grouping or repeated subtraction

Here are two examples showing this way of seeing division.

(i) There are 6 apples, how many groups of 2 are there?

Or, how many 2s make 6?

You can find this out by grouping the apples into twos. There are 3 groups. Or, by taking away two at a time, you find there are 3 such groups.

To work this out we calculate the division: 6 ÷ 2 = 3.

(ii) How many tens are there in 80?

To work this out we calculate 80 ÷ 10 = 8.

Using these examples as a basis, you can help enormously by doing lots of practical work with your child using everyday items. You can help them learn their multiplication and division facts:

1 × 2 = 2	2 ÷ 2 = 1
2 × 2 = 4	4 ÷ 2 = 2
"	"
"	"
10 × 2 = 20	20 ÷ 2 = 10 (Year 2)

Vocabulary

There are many expressions used to mean work out a division. Here are some:

- Halve (means divide by 2)
- Divide
- Share
- Equal groups of . . .

Workout 12

1. Share 16 chocolates between 2. (Year 2)
2. How many tens make 40? (Year 2)
3. How many £2 coins do you get for £12? (Year 2)

Data handling: bar charts, pie charts, etc.

What is data handling?

We are constantly making decisions as we go about our lives. For example, is it safe to cross the road? To make that decision, we need information – in this case, is the road clear? That information is found out by looking out for traffic, or any other hazards that affect our safety crossing the road.

Looking out for hazards is what we could call collecting data. Once we have enough data we then subconsciously make sense of it, and then make a decision to cross the road or not. If, for example, the road is not clear because there is a bus approaching, we know from experience that this is dangerous and we do not cross the road. We have actually handled and sorted a lot of data to give us the information we required to make that decision.

Professionals such as medical doctors see symptoms (data) and use these together with their knowledge to form the information required to make decisions on treatments.

In business, the data about customers' shopping habits helps form the information needed to make decisions about what to stock, etc.

You can see the idea from these examples that we start with raw data, which is organized and sorted so that it makes sense and gives us useful information so that a decision can be made.

This process, from collecting data to making a decision, is known as data handling.

How data handling is taught in schools

Children start learning about data handling in Year 1, at first organizing and using data in very practical situations.

In Year 1, a typical example is to find out how many cubes their friends can hold in one hand. They would discuss questions such as how can you find this out? Then they would carry out an experiment and write down the results. How can the results be shown so that they can easily answer questions such as who holds the most cubes?

One way would be to display the data using a table, as shown here:

Name	Number of cubes
Joe	7
Mary	5
Adam	8
Sara	6

From the table, we can see that Adam holds the most, and Mary the least.

As children progress, they learn more ways to display data, and how to tackle more challenging tasks. Here are some examples of ways to display data:

1. A pictogram, where ☺ represents one child. (Year 1)

2. Colours of cars in the staff car park.

Here is a bar chart. The lengths of the bars show how many cars are in each colour category. A bar chart like this could be used to answer the question, 'What do you think is the most popular colour car in the staff car park?'

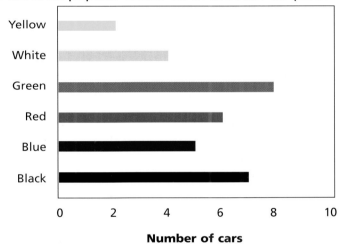

Number of cars

Much later on, about Year 6, children learn about interpreting data using what is known as pie charts, where it is easier to see proportions at a glance.

For example, the above information about colours of cars in the staff car park would look like this (below) using a pie chart, where it is easy to see that about $1/4$ of the cars were green.

The use of ICT is also common for displaying data.

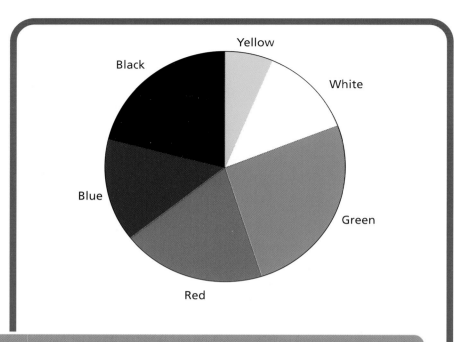

Helping your child

As a parent, helping your child to develop the logic behind the basic data handling skills is easily done as it is very much part of everyday life. For example, finding out what drink their friends want when visiting is a data handling exercise. Planning a party, a trip out, making shopping lists, etc. are other examples.

Have fun developing this area together!!

Measuring

By the time students are 6 to 7 years old, some time in Year 2, they would be using metres and centimetres to measure lengths, kilograms and grams to weigh objects and litres and millilitres to measure the capacity of containers. For example, a jug is filled and students would read off the scale on the side of the jug to find out how many millilitres of water are in the jug. These units are known as metric measurements.

Before they start on this kind of work, there are many easy, everyday activities your child can do with you to help them to understand the background concepts and ideas and so be confident in this area.

Background

When we are measuring we are in effect comparing our item with some standard unit of measure. Historically, all sorts of units have been used. Here are some: a cubit is the length from the elbow to the tip of your middle finger; a hand span, the length from the end of the little finger of a hand spread out to the tip of the thumb.

The trouble is, people all have different personal measurements for these, and so for fairness, we need a standard length so we all know what we are talking about.

We used to use imperial units: feet and inches to measure length, pounds and ounces to weigh objects and pints and gallons to measure capacity. As some parts of the world (e.g. USA) still use imperial units, and they are still used in everyday conversations, children do learn about these too; but the focus is on metric measurements and they are the standard units we use.

We use many words and phrases to compare items, and you can help your child grasp these so that when faced with word problems, they will more easily understand what is needed.

Before they start school, you can help them understand basic ideas such as what is meant by: deep and shallow (look at puddles!); near and far (look at buildings along a road, which is near and which is far away?); who is shortest? (stand back to back with a friend); the idea of full and empty, then half-full. While helping putting away shopping, take two objects, say a packet of biscuits and a tin of beans – which feels heavier?

How measuring is taught in schools

In schools children learn how to use both uniform non-standard units (e.g. estimating then finding out how many matchsticks would fit across a book) and standard units (e.g. estimating then using a ruler marked in centimetres to measure and compare objects).

They start off using metres, then learn about smaller units (centimetres) and the connection between them; in a similar way, kilograms and grams, and litres and millilitres.

They learn that:

1 metre (m)	= 100 centimetres (cm)
1 kilogram (kg)	= 1000 grams (g)
1 litre (l)	= 1000 millilitres (ml) (Year 2)

A lot of practical work is carried out in lessons. Activities include weighing objects using balances and weights to find which is heaviest, finding out which of a number of containers holds the most/least by filling them and counting how many cups of water each holds.

How to help

At this stage, the basic skill of how to measure lengths correctly and read scales accurately is very important. Helping them to know how to use a ruler to make accurate measurements by checking that they start measuring from the correct place on a ruler, is a very important way you can help as some children find this confusing. Estimating, for example, which mug do you think holds the most water, and then checking, is an important skill in this area and you can help in this as you go about your everyday life with your child. Get to know

with your child how long 1cm, 10cm, 1m looks like.
Another way to help is by together weighing out
ingredients for cooking. And when you are putting away
shopping, let them help and talk about heavier and
lighter items.

Lastly, they need to realize that even though the units are
different, we solve problems using the usual methods of
addition, subtraction, multiplication and division.

Workout 13

1. The lounge is 8m long. The hall is 5m long. The
    lounge is longer than the hall. How much longer?
    (Year 1)

2. A full jug holds 5 cups of juice. How many cups of
    juice do 2 full jugs hold? (Year 1)

3. My tomato plant is 50cm tall. Sara's is 30cm taller.
    How tall is Sara's plant? (Year 2)

Money

Money is a very important part of our everyday life, and being able to handle it successfully is a skill that everyone needs.

To start with we need to recognize and understand our currency: pounds (£) and pence (p). We need to recognize all the coins and notes and appreciate their value.

We need to know that 100p = £1 and that we can exchange every 100 pence with a £1 coin.

So 132p is £1 and 32p. We write this as £1.32, and 508p is £5 and 8p written as £5.08. In other words:

132p = £1.32, and 508p = £5.08.

Then we need to know how to calculate the total bill, and then how to use suitable notes and coins to pay, and give

change. We need to know whether an item is more expensive than another item. We do this by comparing prices and mentally calculating which price is larger and by how much.

There is plenty of scope for you to help your child develop these skills as you go about your daily life together shopping and paying for things. You can start off by showing them a handful of small change and explain what each coin is worth.

How problems involving money are taught in schools

As we have seen, to start with it is important for children to recognize the coins and appreciate their value. They learn this in Year 1 and Year 2 by having plenty of practice of exchanging coins for similar values. Having found totals, they need to learn about the possible combinations of coins that can be used to pay.

Workout 14

1. Ali spent 6p, what was her change from 10p?
   (Year 1)

2. Describe different ways of paying exactly 8p.
   (Year 1)

3. Which three coins make (i) 9p (ii) 13p? (Year 1)

4. Exchange this 50p coin for three coins of the same total value. (Year 2)

5. How many pence in £1.75? (Year 2)

6. (i) What is the total cost of a pencil at 15p and a sharpener at 20p?

   (ii) What five coins could I use to pay for this exactly? (Year 2)

Vocabulary

Children need to understand the meaning of certain words to do with money, such as: price, change, total, cost, cost more/less. Some time in Year 2 they start to use the symbol £.

In Year 3 they start to recognize the value of £5, £10 and £20 notes and, for example, exchange a note for the equivalent value in £1, £2 coins.

They need to know how to calculate the cost, and work out the change, find the price, which costs more/less and by how much.

How you can help

You can help them understand the key ideas in handling money. For example, help them work out how much change from 50p they get. They can use the shopkeepers' method (see Subtraction and Addition). Later on, they can use compensating when adding together totals such as £3.99 and £4.99 (see Addition and Subtraction). Have fun together practising important mental arithmetic addition skills!

 Workout 15

1. Bananas cost 12p each.

   (i) How much do two bananas cost?

   (ii) What four coins can I use to pay for them exactly?   (Year 1)

2. A pencil costs 14p, a pen is 15p more.

   (i) What does a pen cost?

   (ii) I buy a pen, how much change is there from 50p?   (Year 2)

3. Write in £ and pence the total of 5 £1 coins and 32 pence.   (Year 2)

4. What is a half of £22?   (Year 2)

Time

We take time for granted, but actually it is very complicated as there are a number of things that are important for children to understand even before any calculations are attempted. You can help with these even before your child comes to school.

First, there is the vocabulary associated with time. They start off with knowing the names of the days of the week (Reception), and being aware that the day is split up into morning, afternoon and night. Children also need to be aware that time is a non-metric measure, in other words, we do not count in 10s and 100s. For example, a digital clock now showing 8:59 in three minutes will show 9:02 not 8:62.

There are:

7 days in a week (not 10)

24 hours in a day

60 minutes in an hour

60 seconds in a minute.

These facts are gradually introduced to the children as they progress through school, and we shall see the progression through Key Stage 1.

Then children need to read and know the time, and begin to be able to judge how long things take to do. These last two are very important practical skills for everyday life.

Then, of course, they need to be able to perform calculations.

How time is taught in schools

To start with, in Reception, children begin to use vocabulary associated with time, e.g. know the days of the week in order, and to read the o'clock time. They begin to know the time of key events in the day, e.g. school finishes at 3 o'clock. They begin to learn how to put the events of their day in sequence. This is done, for example, by ordering picture cards to tell a story. To get a feel for the duration of time, they may be asked, 'Can you pack away the pencils before I count to 10?' They may listen to stories such as *The Very Hungry Caterpillar* by Eric Carle.

You can help by using words such as yesterday and tomorrow in conversations. For example, ask, 'Who came to visit yesterday?' to help them understand the meaning of these words.

In Year 1 they learn:

1 week   = 7 days

1 day   = 24 hours

and the use of the comparatives faster and slower. They read the time to the hour and half-hour using an analogue clock. They learn about the seasons: spring, summer, autumn and winter, and use of expressions such as, How long will it be to . . . ?

In Year 2 they learn about the months of the year and their correct order. They also learn:

1 hour   = 60 minutes

1 minute   = 60 seconds

and how to read time to hour, half- and quarter-hours using both digital and analogue clocks.

We can say the times on these clocks are a quarter to 8, or we can say 15 minutes to 8, or we can say it is seven forty-five.

As you can see, children gradually learn to tell the time more and more accurately as they get older. In schools, it is not until Year 3 that children learn to use 'am' and 'pm'.

You can help by showing them the display on electrical appliances and on analogue clocks/watches to help them see that they are the same, and practise telling the time using both.

1. How long is it from 2 o'clock to 5 o'clock? (Year 1)

2. It is now half-past 8. What time was it 2 hours ago? (Year 1)

3. What day comes after Friday? (Year 1)

4. What time will it be 2 hours after 4 o'clock? (Year 2)

5. Write the time in two ways.

6. What month comes before July?

Appendix 1: Multiplication square

Here is a multiplication square showing all the times tables up to 10 × 10.

×	1	2	3	4	5	6	7	8	9	10
1	1	2	3	4	5	6	7	8	9	10
2	2	4	6	8	10	12	14	16	18	20
3	3	6	9	12	15	18	21	24	27	30
4	4	8	12	16	20	24	28	32	36	40
5	5	10	15	20	25	30	35	40	45	50
6	6	12	18	24	30	36	42	48	54	60
7	7	14	21	28	35	42	49	56	63	70
8	8	16	24	32	40	48	56	64	72	80
9	9	18	27	36	45	54	63	72	81	90
10	10	20	30	40	50	60	70	80	90	100

Using the fact that multiplication and division are inverse operations, we can use the square to calculate divisions too.

Highlighted is:

$3 \times 4 = 12$.

We can also use the same highlighted squares to work out that:

$12 \div 4 = 3$ and $12 \div 3 = 4$.

Students use the square in this way in about Year 5.

Try using it for yourself to check your multiplication and division facts.

Appendix 2: Targets and resources

I have discussed in each section how each topic mentioned in the book is taught in schools, and the progression through Key Stage 1 is outlined. These targets give you a gist of the sort of things your child should be able to do by the end of the school year. They are not intended as a complete summary!!

Reception

- Reliably count up to ten
- Using the numbers from 1 to 10, be able to find one more/one less
- Understand the meaning of words such as more or less, heavier or lighter, greater or smaller when comparing say two numbers or quantities

Year 1

- Reliably count up to 20
- Know all the pairs of numbers with a total of 10
- Be able to put the numbers 0 to 20 in order
- Solve simple problems mentally by counting on, doubling and halving, and be able to explain their methods orally

- Count, read, write and put into order numbers up to 100

- Be able to count on, or back, in ones or tens from any two-digit number

- Be able to use a ruler to draw and measure lines to the nearest centimetre

- Know their 2 and 10 times tables by heart

Some schools have been sending home Parent Booklets that give a list of numeracy targets for your child for the year, and give ideas of how to help your child with mathematics. You can download these for yourself at:

http://www.standards.dfes.gov.uk/primary/publications/mathematics/12792/

Useful resources

Here are some useful resources that I can recommend which can also be used to help your child with numeracy.

The government has a very useful website for parents, which gives a list of the targets for your child in a number of subjects. You can see this at:

http://www.parentscentre.gov.uk/learnjourn/index_ks1.cfm ?ver=graph&subject=ma&subpage=targets&tip=intro

The BBC has some very good numeracy games and activities that are suitable for supporting your child's work in maths. You can see these on their website:

http://www.bbc.co.uk/schools/parents/search/

Appendix 3: Glossary

Array

This is an organized arrangement of objects.

Decimals or Decimal Fractions

Decimals, or decimal fractions to give them their full name, are fractions with denominators 10, 100, 1000, etc. We use a special notation to write these fractions, called decimal notation, and write $^1/_{10}$ as 0.1, $^1/_{100}$ as 0.01, etc.

Denominator

See fractions.

Fractions

In everyday life, we use the word fraction to mean something smaller. For example, 'I bought this belt at a fraction of the price' – means that you have got a bargain, and paid a smaller price than usual. Fractions have a similar meaning in mathematics except when you split something into fractions, either an item such as a cake, or an amount such as 30p, you split whatever you start with into smaller equal parts. Halving is splitting the something into two equal parts; splitting into thirds means splitting the something into three equal parts.

We use special symbols to show a fraction.

A half is written $^1/_2$. The bottom number (the denominator) tells you the number of equal parts, the top number (the numerator) tells you the number of these equal parts you want.

Inverse Operations

These are operations that reverse or 'undo' the original operation.

Division and multiplication are what are known as inverse operations. Addition and subtraction are also inverse operations.

For example, with addition and subtraction, starting with 4, then add 3, we get 7. But, 7 minus 3 gets us back to 4, the number we started with. The subtraction undoes the addition.

Written out, it looks like this: $4 + 3 = 7$, and $7 - 3 = 4$.

The same happens with division and multiplication. If we start with 3 multiplied by 4 we get 12. If we divide 12 by 4 we get 3, the number we started with.

Written out, it looks like this: $3 \times 4 = 12$, and $12 \div 4 = 3$.

Numerator

See fractions.

Partitioning

This is splitting a number into 100s, 10s and units, etc. For example, twelve is a ten and a two, or $12 = 10 + 2$.

Appendix 4: Workout answers

Workout 1

1. (i) 8 (ii) 16 (iii) 7

2. (i) 70 (ii) 30

3. Check by counting with them

Workout 2

1. 72

2. 156

3. 306

4. 914 (Remember fourteen is our way of saying a ten and a four)

Workout 3

1. 1 × 10p coin and 8 × 1p coins

2. (i) 80 (ii) 4

3. (i) 500 (ii) 30

4. Biggest 832, smallest 238

5. 8756

6. They represent 50 and 6

Workout 4

1. 23

2. 48

3. 81 tens

Workout 5

2. 11, 12, 13, 14, 15, 16

3. 22mm, 15mm, 12mm, 8mm, 4mm

4. £2.20, £2.50, £3.30, £5.80, £8.80

5. E.g. Start with largest number 59 + 30 + 1 + 2 = 92

Workout 6

1. 7

2. 12

3. (i) 17 (ii) e.g. 12 + 8 = 20

4. 190

5. 17

Workout 7

```
(i)      58        58          (ii)     765        765
       + 35      + 35                  + 73       + 73
       ----      ----                  ----       ----
         13        93                     8        838
       ----                            ----       ----
         80         1                   130          1
       ----                            ----
         93                            700
       ----                            ----
                                       838
                                       ----
```

Workout 8

These would be illustrated using suitable number lines.

Workout 9

£4.99 + £7.99 = £5 − 1p + £8 − 1p = £13 − 2p = £12.98

Workout 10

1. $\frac{1}{2}$

2. 2 nuts should be ringed off

3. The two parts are not equal

4. (i) One block is shaded. (ii) $\frac{9}{10}$

Workout 11

1. 16

2. 16

3. 80

4. 8cm

Workout 12

1. 8 chocolates each (16 ÷ 2 = 8)

2. 4 (40 ÷ 10 = 4)

3. 6 (12 ÷ 2 = 6)

Workout 13

1. 3m

2. 10 cups

3. 50cm + 30cm = 80cm

Workout 14

1. 4p

2. 4 × 2p; 8 × 1p; a 5p, a 2p and a 1p; a 5p, and 3 × 1p; etc.

3. (i) a 5p and 2 × 2p (ii) a 10p, a 1p and a 2p

4. 2 × 20p and a 10p

5. 175p

6. (i) 35p (ii) 2 × 10p and 3 × 5p; a 20p, a 10p, 2 × 2p and a 1p

Workout 15

1. (i) 24p (ii) 2 × 10p and 2 × 2p; a 20p, a 2p and 2 × 1p

2. (i) 29p (ii) 21p

3. £5.32

4. £11

Workout 16

1. 3 hours

2. Half-past 6

3. Saturday

4. 6 o'clock

5. 5:45, or a quarter to 6, or 15 minutes to 6

6. June

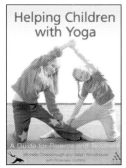